HEAL *the* BOY
BUILD *the* MAN

SHAWN T. MCINTYRE

To contact Shawn: www.ShawnTMcIntyre.com

ISBN: 978-1-989849-04-0

DEDICATION

This book is dedicated to my five beautiful daughters, they have always been my reason to want to become better and my 'why' to transform.

To my one son who has shown me so many parts within me, in order to love and embrace so I can show up fully for him.

To my amazing wife for believing in me and showing me all the challenges were so worth it.

Also, to my special mom who has guided me from the boy to the man and has always been in my heart and soul.

Love you all, Shawn.

TABLE OF CONTENTS

FOREWORD

THE READ OF YOUR LIFETIME

Over the past 12 years, it's been a joy to mentor Shawn T. McIntyre as he grew tremendously in business from building to selling a firm he founded. I've been delighted to watch Shawn start with a dream as a young man entering body building competitions, to thriving as he holds a World Champion Status year-after-year in this demanding sport.

I have watched Shawn succeed in his personal life as a father, a husband, and as a leader, so it's no wonder that Shawn's now expanding his dreams to help others win and succeed by sharing what he knows around that it takes to have a mindset of winning leadership; to truly go for your deepest desires.

Inside these pages you will discover the "missing pieces" needed to heal and develop the whole self. What Shawn defines is principles he discovered, that ultimately created a simple change in his thinking which lead to better disciplines to handle any challenge and obstacle in becoming Unstoppable.

Berny Dohrmann
Founder of CEO Space

ACKNOWLEDGMENTS

Although writing a book seems to be an individual endeavour, it is really a coming together of many helping hands, insights and a team to bring this vision into reality.

I'd first like to thank my beautiful wife Jessica for all the very long, early and late hour discussions dedicated to bring this book to life.

To all my children Ashley, Haley, Sophie, Jenna, Theo-James and Victoria thank you for all your support and allowing me the space to do my true work and passion. It is my true wish to see you all pursue your dreams and purpose.

To my mom Karen, thank you for your endless love and constant support. To my step dad Eldon for demonstrating in life that our dreams matter and do come true!

Next I'd like to thank Karen Michele West for all the conversations to edit and bring this book into reality. To Kelly Falardeau and Carrie Kohan for all your encouragement and support.

I am grateful for my mentorship with the late Berny Dohrmann and September Dohrmann for your friendship and teachings from the very beginning. Thank you Lindsey Andersen and Adam Norton for your guidance and support. Also Norisa Anderson for the great cover, captioning my son and I. It was so much fun to have my son Theo on the cover as the younger version of me.

We cannot achieve anything alone; I am so thankful to my brothers, ex wives and business partners for playing your parts perfectly for my life to develop and unfold. Finally, to my entire team and community to create this for thousands and hopefully millions to read!

Shawn T. McIntyre

INTRODUCTION

May you find this book pivotal and life changing for your own personal transformation. Through the sharing of my stories you can gain valuable insight as to who you are and what your life is truly about. No matter where you are right now, whatever your gender, religion, sexual preference, age or race; I hope these stories will resonate and inspire you to level up. It is my goal, that together we can see you move from merely surviving to ultimately thriving. I want you to experience your true nature in its full expression.

Life doesn't come with an owner's manual, because if it had, believe me, I would have certainly read it. An owner's manual will not get you maximum performance from this life, only you can.

What you need is an immense desire to unleash your purpose which is so much bigger than you.

This transformation will have a have a ripple effect inspiring others to transform. The change we want to see in the world can only come from personal transformation by building a better you!

I will take you on my journey of self-discovery and show you how in the face of every challenge, you have the personal choice to rise up and conquer any fears holding you back and keeping you down. By sharing a few puzzle pieces from my intimate stories, it will give you insight as to how I became the man I am today. Some of my darkest moments were; going through a second divorce, being broke, stressed out beyond belief and bed ridden. I was in a single room apartment where I was just trying to take care of my daughters that I faced my biggest fears all at once, and not only survived, but lived to thrive on in spite of the challenges! I was able to stand up in all areas of my life and take on whatever came my way after 38 years of being stuck and struggling.

Each one of us has a purpose to fulfill in our lifetime coming from the seed planted within. I knew because of the struggles and challenges I would be better off for it in the end. At this point in my life, I want to help others embrace and embark on their own personal journey, to realize their full potential with passion and purpose and be able to share it with others. Inside each of us is the seed of greatness, let's call it your level 10 that is simply lying dormant. It contains the desire and blueprint to become boundless in creating a most powerful and unstoppable life. Just like the acorn came with everything to become its destiny of the mighty oak tree, the same is true for you. I want to stir and ignite that desire within. It's now time to wake up, lose the excuses and get real together.

Far too many people are experiencing life like the walking dead in a zombie movie. Barely existing and aimlessly bumbling through life is not living at all, and it creates so much needless suffering. Some people even believe that it is easier to quit and give away their power; that couldn't be farther from the truth. Your soul's desire to fully express itself will never let up, and neither will your suffering if you try to suppress or stop it.

Take it from me, it's much easier to jump into life with both feet, put the pedal to the metal per se and just go full throttle into experiencing everything you can. Yup, bumps and bruises are coming your way for sure and that is where the growing is. It is the challenges and the way you handle them that will shape you, make you and take you to your life's level 10. Do not side step opportunities and life experiences to grow, or you will remain stagnant.

Our world is changing faster than ever with technologies, global economies, politics and even pandemics. It's overwhelming to many, which is leading to depression and complete system shut down. The unrest and differences between us have become magnified where survival of the fittest is once again threatening to wreak havoc; there is so much uncertainty and anxiety. Now more than ever, it is imperative you draw from the power within and rise up in your life and become your own superhero. No one else is coming to save you!

Our societies have made it way too easy to just numb the suffering and become addicted with food, drugs, alcohol, technology, shopping etc. It's alarming how the rate of suicide is increasing and out of control. It's your responsibility to discover your purpose that resides within you. From the moment of conception, this purpose inside has wanted to come through you and be fully realized in this world. By not stepping up, we run the risk of falling into traps of numbing and avoiding. Where is the living in that, I ask you? We came here to grow, expand and go for the dreams of our soul in this life adventure. It is important to expand and experience all that we can by reaching and stretching beyond any limited thinking or belief system. Life will challenge you and develop you until you step into your purpose, even if it has to take you to your knees to get your attention. This is a good thing.

So, how do we be the eye of the storm and enjoy the calm amongst all this chaos and tribulation? How can we achieve financial success, happiness, love, health and abundance? Ultimately we embrace it, that's what we do, and we go deep inside ourselves to find the calm, peace and certainty we need to go forward in spite of whatever is happening around us. The answers have never been outside yourself, the solution is to bring forward the wisdom within you like a unique fingerprint to unlock the genius inside.

You are not alone on this journey, we are all part of this human ecosystem connected to one another to fulfill our life's purpose. Putting each other through the fire is one way we crack open the seed of purpose and allow transformation to happen. I am going to share with you the struggles in my life and how I was able to tap in to the unknown and unseen power within, this allowed me to live my true authentic life at a level 10. I am also going to help you understand how chaos leads to clarity and how getting out of your own way is easier than you think. If you are on board, let's get to it shall we?

PHASE 1

REVEALING *the* BOY

Chapter 1

WHY LIVING YOUR PURPOSE
IS NECESSARY

You've been entrusted to ensure what has been planted within you develops and it is your responsibility to make sure it happens in this lifetime. To fully awaken, you must first understand how perhaps, you have fallen asleep and forgotten the purpose of your own life. The lure and believing that the outside physical plane is our only reality is the bait that traps us into unconscious living. Without connection to our purpose, everything becomes meaningless and naturally falls away. It is only when you awaken to your purpose can you really ever have it all. I believe that you can have your cake and eat it too! This path is not for the faint of heart. It is a journey to where champions are made. It is for those who are willing, to challenge their present day reality by changing their mindset in order to have the life they were destined for. No guts, no glory, end of story!

The quote "Life is like a river, you can never touch the same water twice, so when it feels right, jump in!" is a great calling to all of us, no matter where we are right now, wouldn't you agree? If you recognize that something is missing, or you are dissatisfied with things as they are, now may be a good time to jump in on the path of awakening and transformation with me. Come on in, the water is great! Well, that's how I see it anyway.

Chapter 2

SHAWN'S SHORE - SEEING BENEATH THE SURFACE OF LIFE!

Let me tell you about Shawn's Shore, becoming a fish whisperer at the age of eight years old and developing one or two elements of self-mastery in the process. From early childhood I have felt an inseparable connection to nature. In fact, I could have been called the Nature Boy.

I loved the summertime and being at my grandparent's cabin at the lake. It was so exhilarating to be down at the lake shore with my fishing rod. At five thirty in the morning, feeling completely connected to life. In the tranquility of those mornings, I could go within and seek answers to so many questions about fishing and life. Somewhere, out of nowhere, answers would just seep into my mind and provide me with much needed wisdom and support. It was just natural and normal.

The night before, I would organize my tackle box and fishing rods with great care and intent. The next morning, I would head to my favourite spot and survey the weather conditions and take notice of wind direction and speed, sunny or cloudy and time of day. I would cast out my line and counted as my favourite baited hook drifted down – one, two, three, four and when my line went slack, I knew I had hit the bottom. Through this, I learned, if I counted to ten, the lake was approximately ten feet deep in that spot. Next, I would reel my hook in very slowly to see with my mind's eye and chart the way back shore and create that mental map. This mental map was the secret.

For me, fishing was a connection to nature and being in union with everything. By the end of summer, I had a full journal logged of where and when I caught these fish, the feeding patterns, and even the nature of the fish under many different conditions. Through every cast and reel day after day, I had a mental map of the lake, that would put any fish finder to shame. That being said, that journal also included the story of my life. In those pages were thoughts, feelings and emotions that rose up out of me in order to have clarity and resolution.

In the community, I became known as the Fish Whisperer of Shawn's Shore because of the treasure trove of fish the lake seemed to effortlessly give me. The awestruck neighbours eagerly began to get up earlier and earlier to move in and stand closer to me hoping to learn my secret. Of course, the lake never gave up what it gave to me, no matter how hard they tried. My secret was safe, but the secret was, there was no secret. Others simply missed what I paid attention to. The hidden from sight subtleties of the rocks, ledges and weed patches on the lakebed below. The time of day, weather and seasons all allowed me to match the patterns to the conditions and create an adaptable strategy that worked every time. Like magic, I could pull in multiple fish in the same area, same time of day without them getting so much as a bite. I paid attention to the smallest details and had a laser like focus which allowed me to completely zone in. It wasn't long after, I started getting offers to guide people and take them fishing. By mastering this one shore, I had in fact, mastered the entire lake. It all boiled down to consistency, discipline, paying attention and patience. This is as true in fishing as it is in life. It's all about being connected.

Shawn's Shore is where I learned what it takes to master one thing, but also be able to transfer that mastery into all other aspects of life. I learned to see with my mind's eye and intuition, rather than just my physical eyes, far beneath the reflection and the water's surface and into the depths of the world and life below. This mastery of seeing beyond and deeper from within versus seeing what is visible at the surface, applies to all aspects of our life. Confidence comes from clarity of purpose and success comes from doing the work and paying attention. I also need to mention the importance of getting up early. As the saying goes "Early to bed and early to rise makes you healthy, wealthy and wise".

Chapter 3

THE STRUGGLES OF AN EXTERNALLY FOCUSED LIFE

As a child growing up, wanting to be accepted, approved of and unconditionally loved; I often felt abandoned, alone and very much afraid. Completely unaware that everything I needed was already planted inside me, I would look for ways to prove myself to feel accepted and that I was enough, just as I was. What ultimately led me to give away my personal power was seeking approval and acceptance from everything outside of myself, little by little until I felt empty inside. The pain and agony of the hollowness I felt inside made me desperate to fill it up at any cost. Had I known then, everything I needed to be fulfilled at a level 10 was already within me.

My early childhood wounding and programming began right on schedule, as it does for all of us. For me, this started at the age of one year old, it was right after my dad left us. Later on, I would discover what a great loss this was in my life. I was terrified my mom would leave as well, which is why to cope with this anxiety and fear, I learned to become a people pleaser so no one would abandon or harm me. I hated when my mom had to go to work or school and I was left in the care of my two older brothers who didn't know how to take care of me. They took their own frustrations out on me and used me as a punching bag because of their childhood wounds. For them the loss of our father must have been traumatizing. In the process, I tried to stay out of their way, all the while yearning to be with them as their little brother. This taught me valuable survival skills.

My life growing up with my brothers was a bitter sweet experience. From my earliest memories of my life, I always remember looking up to my brothers. I wanted to be included and do everything with them and to be just like them. They seemed to get all the attention from our uncles and grandpa who were the only male role models in our lives. I wanted to be a part of that too. Whenever I was alone with my brothers, bad things always seemed to happen. My first trip to the hospital was when I was two years old, an incident that still haunts my mother to this day.

One of my brothers had pushed me from the couch into the corner of the coffee table on which I struck my head requiring stitches, but this was just the beginning. Many times when playing floor hockey in the basement I got put in net as goalie. As a result of being placed in that position I was ganged up on with pucks and balls being zinged at me and being hit with their sticks.

The basement was truly a scary place because my brothers always had great games like crazy carpeting down the stairs. They would grab me, place me on the sheet and then push me down the stairs. You'd think they would be the first to try it, but that was not the case. When my brothers were home, they often had friends over, and they would either pick on me or ignore me. I am still not sure which one was worse.

I'm sure my mom thought we were loving brothers but I saw it differently. I instinctively knew I was not safe in my own environment and learned to hide in order to avoid pain.

When it came to food, this is where I first started to learn about survival of the fittest. When my mom bought groceries, it was free for all food frenzy. Being last in the pecking order, I always got the leftovers, my brothers always took the good things first. When mom wasn't home to make supper, because she was working and going to school to provide us a better life, my brothers had to make it, and they usually gave me bread, butter and milk, which led to me being malnourished and getting a full body yeast infection. I always felt like I had to fight for anything more than that. When it came to clothing, I got the hand me downs that were worn so thin they had no shape to them and didn't fit me properly. This continued till grade four and I still remember being teased from the kids at school who had nicer clothes.

My first lesson in entrepreneurship came when I was six, my oldest brother had a paper route which made money and I thought that was so cool. He said if I would help him, he would give me a Cadbury Cream Easter egg. I thought this was great, spending time with my brother and getting a treat. I was so innocent and gullible, I didn't realize that I would be doing all the delivery of the papers for this promised Easter egg and he'd collect the money.

I remember being about seven years old and chasing after my brothers on our bikes as we rode to the convenience store. I am sure they were trying to out run me and leave me behind, but I wanted to keep up so I pedalled hard and fast. As I crossed this intersection on my bike, a car didn't see me and I was hit by that car. I remember hitting his hood and bouncing right off it. I frantically looked around and picked up my bike because I couldn't lose my brothers who were way ahead of me by then. I needed to keep going and I remember looking back and seeing the driver standing there in the middle of the road watching me in disbelief with his hands locked behind the back of his head probably wondering what the hell just happened. Looking back on this one incident it's pretty unbelievable that even being hit by a car wasn't going to stop me from trying to fit in and be with my brothers.

When I was in grade four and five, we had access to a swimming pool and my biggest fear was being thrown into the pool cover and suffocating to death. It was just like when I was wrapped in a blanket and tossed down the stairs; it was terrifying.

Several times at the lake in the summer, my brother would shove me out of the boat and into the lake and I remember freaking out until someone pulled me back in. I often wondered why there was no adult intervention. I literally had nightmares no one would save me.

As we approached our teenage years, the torment and rejection only got worse. My brothers would come home from school with their own frustrations and literally for no reason attack me. I would get pushed face first into the corner of cupboards and into glass windows shattering the glass. Despite this, I still tried to be friends, longing only to be accepted. I saw that I had to use my intelligence to make things work for me. Through this, I developed a keen sense of awareness and alertness, which in the end wasn't all that bad, now that I think about it.

It's amazing the stories and lies we create through our childhood experiences. The times I spent with my grandfather on the farm passed on the beliefs, "Life is all work and no play." and "You had to work hard in order to get what you wanted out of life" and if you did get what you wanted, you were damn lucky."

I remember one day, after working alongside him all day, he took me to town and bought me an ice cream. This was a great memory for me, as we sat together, he said to me, "Shawn, this is life, we always work before we play," and he really wanted to instil that principle into me for some reason. Looking back, I can see how these moments convinced me that life was hard and could be no other way. Eventually I would come to see this as a lie. Well, we all know that life doesn't always give us what we want, but it sure serves up big helpings of what we need.

Giving away all my power through belief systems that I created as a child, evolved into patterns and methods of operations for me to live by. This cultivated a painful emptiness and vacuum inside of me. I then began trying to fill that void with things outside of myself. Believing once I fixed the external, I would then have inner peace and confidence that I was frantically pursuing. This created a hunger that could never be satisfied.

We all come into this life to fulfill the ultimate potential and purpose from the blueprint hidden within that seed. The most ironic thing is that when you arrive here, you either forget your purpose or don't even know you have one. This is why you have to go through the awakening process where we become forged in fire through all of our experiences. Possessing all the power to realize our destiny, all we need is the instrument to crack open that inner seed. In this world, that instrument is learning the lessons to discover who we are not, so we can expand into who we truly are. Our process is similar to that of the Jack Pine tree. The Jack Pine produces durable resin-filled cones to hold its seeds. It takes a fire to melt the resin away and allow the seeds to pop out.

Congruent to this example, you need to go through the fire in order to shed beliefs, mind-sets and accumulation of untruths you unknowingly created. The process of awakening is the opposite of school, first you take the tests and then you learn the lessons. At the time, I couldn't understand that the external world was designed to forge and set me on the path of transformation in order to live the life I was designed for.

My conscious search for meaning, began very similar to many others I am sure. One day, my whole life hit a brick wall, jolting me awake from being asleep at the wheel, you could say. The belief systems I had were no longer working; who I thought I was, was simply falling away and my desire to chase anything outside of myself was coming to an end. I finally came to realize that nothing externally was ever going to make me happy no matter what. The awakening could now begin.

As a kid, I was always drawn to the Walt Disney fairy tales with princes and princesses, castles and kingdoms, wizards and witches and all the other characters in search of truth, love, power and adventure. For this reason, my own life became an extreme adventure, searching for those virtues and values. The challenges were the opportunities to wake up and go beyond any limitations holding me back. There have been epic rises in success and just as many epic failures in for me to discover and embrace my true power in the trifecta of mind, body and spirit. Being able to connect and harness this power is what allowed me to rise out of the ashes and onto the path I was destined for.

Chapter 4

THE LIES WE TELL OURSELVES

Awareness from the awakening process is what led me to boldly seek out and uncover my truth. I needed to understand the lies and more importantly, the whys behind them to come to an acceptance. I decided to embark on an enormous archeological soul search to uncover that seed within. I began excavating those pivotal moments, crucial events and significant consequences. I then came to understand how I abandoned the joy and innocence of a child who became entangled with lies. With every mask I wore, I began to think I was becoming more powerful in the external world. I was actually losing my connection and power from within. These lies cloaked my fears and insecurities. I exhumed a few events that gave me impeccable insight into how I dealt with the feelings and perception that led me to create the stories I told to myself. From these stories, lies were founded, belief systems born and patterns that would become my method of operation all through my youth and into adulthood.

I believe my dad leaving when I was one year old was the earliest and most pivotal incident that set the awakening process in motion for me. The crazy thing is, it wasn't until age five when I first felt the full impact of his abandonment. Up until that point, I was unaware of his absence in my life. It was when I went to kindergarten; my experience of life would take on a whole new meaning, causing me to fall asleep, lose my identity, create masks, blindfolds and facades to cope with my life going forward.

I still remember that first day of kindergarten and feeling nervous from the start. That day, the teacher called a gathering in a circle. It was time to share and get to know the other kids by talking about our parents. We were supposed to talk about our 'dads' specifically. I watched as each of my classmates moved into the center of the circle and stated their dad's name and what they did for work. I never knew my dad and I was never in a position where I had to deal with the feelings of being different or less than anyone else. Immediately, I was overwhelmed with unfamiliar feelings and sheer panic. The anxiety increased as I grappled with what do or say when it was my turn. When it was my turn, everything inside of me went into high alert and the alarm was sounding danger danger. I could feel my face ignite with heat and intensify as I awkwardly, and in slow motion crawled to the center of the circle, trembling to my core. Not knowing what to say or do, I just looked at my classmates and teacher in an awkward gaze. It seemed like an eternity before she broke the painful silence, directing and coaxing me along. She said "Shawn, tell us your name, what your dad's name is, and what he does for work."

I froze and remained silent from the shock and awe of this new awareness, a secret that was kept from me about my father. I could feel a rock in my throat and tightening in the pit of my stomach, which also made it hard to breathe. This led to the other kids laughing and mocking me. The teacher's voice sounded like I was under water, hearing the slow muffled murmur of "Shawn are you ok, is there something wrong?" In a split second after that, a notion to end my suffering popped into my head. I broke the silence and stated that my dad was a detective and I made up a really cool name for him. Immediately, the laughter and mocking from the other kids turned into spectacular awe and praise, which filled me with immense acknowledgement and approval; more importantly, self-confidence.

I had a great sense of relief as I shifted my inner pain to a newfound power and ability to control my outside experiences. For a five year old kid, that is pretty awesome I'd say. By lying, I learned how to control and manipulate external situations in order to avoid dealing with the feelings, emotions and perceptions internally. Just like that, I went from worst to first with one simple lie that flowed out of my mouth and off my tongue so easily.

At the age of seven, I finally got my first bike which I had hoped would be one of my best days ever. Being from a broken family that struggled for money, my bike came from my grandpa's farm. Even though it was an old girl's bike, I was so happy and accepted it joyfully, knowing it could bring me a new sense of freedom and independence. In the next few days; while I was proudly riding my bike, my friends started to ridicule and humiliate me for riding a girl's bike. This ruthless taunting caused me to feel a deep shame and self-loathing inside. It was another pivotal moment where I wanted things to be different so I didn't have to suffer. From that experience, sparked an intense desire to play hockey like my brothers, to prove myself every bit a boy and wear a new mask. It was challenging trying to overcome the limited financial circumstances that I found myself in, but I was able to scrounge enough old give away equipment and skates, to join the team. I didn't have a proper hockey duffle bag because the only thing we could afford were garbage bags. While getting off the city bus one day to play hockey, my bag dragged on the floor and ripped a big hole in the bottom of it. To my horror, all my equipment spilled out onto the stairs and floor of the bus for all the world to see. I burst into tears from the agonizing frustration and inability to control my circumstances. I am sure somewhere in this moment I told myself a few lies, made up some excuses and vowed to find my place in this world by not standing out but by being outstanding!

I decided I was never going to be found lacking anywhere in my life again. The die was cast yet again, and the awakening process continued on. The childhood connection to my own purpose and inner strength began to dissolve away, as the external world hypnotically drew me in with the promise of self-confidence and acceptance. Unaware that my low self-esteem would lead me on such a treacherous path, I carried on trying to fit in and assimilate myself into the outside world. I became a great storyteller, liar and wearer of many masks and blindfolds that I created on the way. Whew! What a ride.

Looking back, I see the wisdom in the process of discovering who I was not, to know the truth of myself and fully heal. I needed to learn from all the lies and the whys behind them. There were often times that seemed quite negative and harsh. In hindsight I now see how the unfolding process was perfect in its design.

Chapter 5

I TRIED EVERYTHING - WHAT'S MISSING?

As time passed and the world continued to change with me in it, my awakening process continued to unfold, gaining momentum with each passing year. I set out with a hell fire in my belly to prove myself worthy and deserving, wanting nothing more than to overcome my circumstances and conquer my past full of fears, failures and abandonment. I finally possessed the power to ensure everything would be different. I had been dreaming of this for so long, when I could finally take the reins and control the direction of my life. Soon I would discover, no matter what I strove for and achieved, I would always be left feeling unhappy and that something was missing because it was..."I" was missing.

That sense of unfulfillment drove me harder and harder to keep on trying or die. I was consumed by the desire to succeed in every aspect of my life to stay beyond reproach when it came to my value and worth. Little did I know what lay ahead. I pressed on with the heart of a gladiator to honour a vow I had made repeatedly over the years. "Oh my God, this will never happen to me again." I vowed to never feel alone, different or be rejected by anyone. I was tired of running away because I was scared and feeling like a loser. What I wanted now was redemption and to be victorious. This was my battle cry "Oh my God this will never happen to me again."

Growing up in a low-income home and being ostracized for lack of money, I decided to pursue the almighty dollar as a measure of my value and worth. I came to believe money would solve all my problems, all I needed to do was go out and get it. I started my first paper route at the age of ten and worked many jobs along the way in the pursuit of success and money to become a man of worth and respect. I worked hard, fast and furiously, doing anything and everything I could to outrun the feeling of being worthless. When I got the money, cars, houses, job titles and other stuff I strived so hard to get, I still felt empty and the same inside. How could I work so hard and still feel so desperate inside? What was wrong with me?

I had no father and sense of family, my greatest desire was to recreate a perfect family so I could be the father I never had in an attempt to heal the past. I aimed to be a stand-up guy, a 'yes' man, a pleaser and man of my word who honoured his commitments, vows and responsibilities. Externally, I knew how the picture looked, so I set the intention to manifest it. Even though I was married twice and had four daughters in ten years, I still could not get the outside picture to match the vision I held inside my mind.

Over the years I was picked on for being scrawny, awkward and lacking in self-confidence. I set out to fix this torment by getting healthy and in the best shape ever. My intention was to chisel out the preverbal David statue from my own body. Day by day, rep by rep I saw my body transform until it became the image I held in my mind. I competed on fitness model stages and won; I was being offered speaking opportunities, photo shoots and now people were starting to really notice and approve of me. I had finally done it! I mean, really achieved something amazing, yet even all this, it still left me feeling like an imposter because the little boy with all the pain and insecurities was still there. I could see him and feel him. I had built a larger body and lifestyle that the boy inside had not been able to grow into. It was like I was playing dress-up in an older man's closet and life. How could I fix this mess and get my life to work? When could the boy grow into the life I wanted so badly? Was this even possible and if so, what would it take?

No 'thing' ever worked despite many years of trying every 'thing'. I finally came to understand my internal pain could never be healed by anything external, I had to go within! The external experiences are necessary to drive you back inside to reconnect to who you are for your level 10 to fully emerge.

Chapter 6

TAKE BACK YOUR POWER
AND LEVEL UP

To take back your power, self-esteem and confidence, you first need to acknowledge that you, and only you, have been giving it all away. Once you realize and accept this, everything in your life will change when you decide to take it back. We live in a world designed to break us down. I know it sounds crazy, but it's perfect. We need this in order to fulfill our mission and unleash our purpose.

My intention is to share some personal experiences that demonstrate the ways in which you give your power away. Not only do I want you to relate, but to embody them to gain expanded awareness and choose to transform your own life. This world will never be

...ne same when you show up and realize your full potential. This is my greatest wish for you.

Chapter 7

THE BREAKING DOWN PROCESS - LIFE'S WAY OF REVEALING MORE

The process of breaking the 'outer' in order to break inside, often seemed more than I could bear at times. I suffered gut wrenching moments of being terrified, heartbroken and rejected, that always left me exhausted and utterly shattered. Day after day, I lived to face another experience expertly designed to have me question what was wrong with me and why did I come into this world broken? If nothing was wrong with me, why would my father have left and never come back? Surely to God, I must have been the problem somehow. How could the person who should've been there for me just vanish from my life if I was not the problem in some way? With the belief 'I was the problem', and there was something wrong, I became a magnet to misadventure every step of the way. The dominos began to tumble into one another from that kindergarten experience where I felt different by not having a dad. This is also where I began to hate my name. When the kindergarten teacher asked me to say my name, I can see clear as day, me looking down at my name tag and viscerally hating my name. Many times when my name was used, there was an underlying tone of anger or ridicule. I just hated hearing my name from then on.

All along, I tried to fit in and avoid any rejection and torment, but when you have buck teeth that required braces and head gear and then the girl you had a crush on crushes you… I still remember her laughing at me and calling me Bucky Beaver; it's pretty easy to understand why I stopped smiling that day. I had big thick glasses, bad haircuts, plain clothes and the worst case of acne.

You can imagine how I hated to look in the mirror or see any pictures of myself, especially my school pictures. I had ear surgery that left me to heal with about six feet of gauze wrapped around my head in the shape of a light bulb, advertising "Hey, look at me."

I was left with hearing loss in my left ear so I would deliberately sleep on my right side to drown out the sounds of chaos, anger and desperation of a broken home.

My mom worked hard and went to school, so in her absence, my nutrition was poor, so much so, that I wound up with a vicious full body yeast overgrowth that threatened my life. My brothers were often in charge of my nutrition which consisted of milk, bread and butter because it was easy.

I was the kid with a key on a string around my neck who let myself in after school, often times to no one being there. When I was fourteen and wearing my retainer, I had a peanut butter and banana sandwich and the retainer got stuck in the sandwich while I was eating it. Somehow I managed to swallow it and it got stuck in my throat. I must have passed out and when I woke up there was no retainer anywhere to be found. I still wonder if it is still inside of me somewhere. I was really lucky I didn't die that day being home alone.

In school, the opportunity to be accepted and nurtured was completely nonexistent. My thoughts, personality and needs were snuffed out by the expectation to conform and be assimilated, even though, I clearly did not fit in. I was obviously a square peg they were trying to shove into a round hole. In the school yard during recess and after school were punishing times for me where my self-esteem and confidence took the most beating. Since I could not be accepted where I wanted to be accepted, I had to try and fit in somewhere. Naturally all that was left, were the rejects, losers and loners. We were always picked on by the other boys and girls because we were deemed weak.

The girls were the worst though, as they could draw out the deepest self-loathing with the proverbial bitch slaps. At the time, there seemed to be nothing worse than being slapped by a girl. I was brought up to believe I could not defend myself or hit girls back when they, brutally kicked me, pulled my hair and said the cruelest things. The physical pain paled in comparison to the agony of being humiliated and helpless to do anything about it.

The one good thing that arose was that I became the lord of the losers. The best of the worst so to speak. There was a part of me though, that almost felt guilty being with them and feeling better about myself. I knew how much it hurt to endure this endless torture. So even though I could not stand up for myself, I could stand up for them; to punch a bully right in the nose for shoving my friend into the lockers.

As long as I was not the center of attention with a target on my back and someone else was weaker than me, I could stand up for them instinctively. I could rise to the occasion because I felt stronger than them. I can still see it in slow motion, how I came between them and watched as my arm drew back and my fist connected to his nose and the blood flowed out. I was immediately scared shitless, but also in a split second, I caught a glimpse that I could fight and win. Being able to rise up was possible in that moment but that realization of how to do that consistently would be forgotten for many more years to come.

At home, my brothers who were three and a half and five years older would unleash their fury, often with their friends in tow. They would wake me up after forcing me to bed early and then torment me by putting clothes pins on my ears, throwing orange juice in my bed and showed me how vulnerable and weak I was. They teased me, called me a loser and beat the crap out of me. I have so many memories of black eyes, scrapes, cuts and needing to go to the hospital for stitches. The thought of seeing that white sheet in the hospital coming down over my head, with the little hole to isolate the area needing to be stitched up just sends shivers down my spine. My mom was traumatized over hearing me cry "Mommy mommy, don't let them do this to me." She told me, even to this day it still haunts her.

In grade seven, being a new kid because we moved from a small town in Saskatchewan to St. Albert, Alberta, the ostracizing intensified. In gym class, we had to wear the ugly purple and yellow shorts provided by the school. The female gym teacher looked at my legs and then commented how much better she felt about her own legs after seeing mine. Hearing that made me want to shrivel up and blow away. It was another moment that caused self-loathing. I also remember sitting in the bleachers with the other guys and comparing our strength by trying to wrap our hands around our thighs. It was really good if your hands didn't touch. My fingers were so long and my thighs were like toothpicks, so I faked that my fingers didn't touch. I had a hard time and simply couldn't fit in with the guys because of all the comparison and competition on who was better, stronger and more popular. When school was done, I walked home by myself feeling very much isolated and alone. At sixteen, my Mom got me a car, like she had done for my older brothers. They received sporty Camaros and Firebirds while I got a four-door jalopy Chevy Nova. I got teased for having a grandma car and felt so embarrassed and had to wonder why I always got the short end of the stick. It was like I was always an afterthought, whether it was hand-me-down clothes, scraps of food or other people's junk. I was mercilessly shamed and singled out because I was six feet two inches and one hundred and fifty pounds that looked like a flagpole.

I began to see the breaking down process was crucial to unlock the next level of becoming who I really am.

Chapter 8

THE PERFECTIONIST – ALWAYS TRYING TO DO THE RIGHT THING

After high school, I was forced to grow up fast as my life took a dramatic turn and I needed to change everything. The belief that I was broken, put in motion the need to strive for perfection as a new way of surviving. Over the years, I took notice of what the world expected, admired and found acceptable. I decided to become all of that and more. I just wanted the opportunity to change it all, right some wrongs and become what I thought everyone expected of me to finally gain approval and fit in. I kept wondering what would my life be like if I could finally be accepted?

Growing up, I had always vowed that when I create my own family, I will never do what my dad did which was to abandon us. Here I was, having to face that vow because at nineteen, I got my girlfriend pregnant and had to make a decision that involved two other lives besides my own. The dilemma, would I stay with her, someone I barely knew, or would I run out on her and my responsibility as a very young father?

I knew I wasn't ready to be a father and I certainly hadn't planned on it, but here I was and with the secret hope I could have someone love, support and believe in me. I felt life was providing me with the opportunity to finally not be alone anymore. But was I ready to be a father? Despite the intense cautioning and concern from family and friends, I decided to honour my vow and man up. How could I not? I was going to be a perfect father, a perfect husband and build a perfect life because this was the chance to do the right thing, and end all the feelings of being alone and abandoned. At that time it seemed less scary to get married and start a family I hadn't planned on. In fact, it seemed better than being alone and having my life continue the way it was.

I was up for the challenge, so I forged ahead and focused on being impeccable in how I presented myself to the world in all aspects. I was quick to pass judgements on myself before anyone else got the chance, to avoid being wrong or found lacking in some way. Facing the challenges that lay ahead of me filled me with a great sense of relief and power because I was finally being given the chance to rise up and win. This need to win was fueled from a fear of failure. In my mind, having a family so young became a shield from being criticized by others, after all, I was the guy who did the right thing. From this at least, I felt I had earned some respect and admiration. I definitely felt I was entitled to a free pass from judgement. How could anyone possibly judge me, they were not in my shoes and if they were, would they have stepped up like I did? It felt like I was a winner.

I was looking for acceptance, connection and to just fit in. By trying to be perfect, I was actually becoming more disconnected to my true self. Unknown to me this was a perfect design to draw me back within and tap into my blueprint so as to continue to build from there.

Chapter 9

THE CHAMELEON – FINDING THE RIGHT FIT

When things didn't work out trying to be perfect, I scrambled to gain some sense of myself again and came up with a new emergency survival strategy. This time I decided I was going to tap into the ultimate camouflage and be like a chameleon so I could adapt, morph and blend into my environments. I needed to protect and prevent, at any cost, the discovery of my low self-esteem and confidence. If I was found out, I just knew it would ruin me. Utilizing my new skills of adapting to just blend in and not be noticed, seemed like it was going to be much easier than working so hard to be perfect and losing myself in the process. Oh, but you know it, I was going to take a beating here in the school of hard knocks for sure. As usual, the g force was to end the pain and suffering inside. I wanted to be accepted because I believed I was unacceptable. What if this time, no one really took notice of me because I could blend in and take the target off my back? Could that be possible? I was intent on finding out.

I was in grade ten and remember growing three or four inches over the summer. I came back to school an awkward and lanky six foot two inch and one hundred and fifty pound bean stalk. I remember being called 'flagpole' that would blow away in the wind and other nasty names. It just seemed that my destiny was to stand out like a sore thumb and be noticed in the most merciless ways.

My clothes never really fit well, and I was at an age where my insecurities continued to mount. I tried everything to avoid being ridiculed and humiliated on a daily basis, but it became impossible. I vowed the same vow I always have and said, "Oh my God, this will never happen to me again!" It is said that desperate people do desperate things and I was about to prove that true. I came up with the idea to buy jeans that were a few sizes larger so I could wear them over top of my sweatpants to make myself look bigger. I also went so far as, to double up my t-shirts under my jean jacket to look more buff and in proportion. I thought if I could just look bigger on the outside, this would give me the camouflage I needed to escape being different and singled out. The good thing was, it worked!

At Christmas break, I experimented in public places like the malls, just moving around in plain sight to see if anyone noticed me and how well I could blend into the crowds without being discovered. I learned how to roll up my sleeves and buy clothes that could be easily layered so it wasn't obvious I was trying to cover up a gangly body underneath.

When school started in the new year, my classmates started paying attention to me and noticed I had really bulked up over Christmas. Finally, this gave me the confirmation to prove this strategy was a success and I had finally found the way to fit in. I enjoyed the newfound attention I was getting from everyone, especially a few of the really popular girls. I finally looked like I fit into my clothes and now the girls started to let me into their inner circle. I still wasn't that popular with the guys, but I was getting invited to all the parties and life was looking up for me, until it wasn't.

At one party, I got jumped by five guys from a different school who literally beat my ass to the pavement. They came out of left field, blindsided me, blackened my eyes and left me with a whole smorgasbord of other injuries. When I got up after they left, I asked my friends "Holy shit! What the hell just happened?"

They didn't know, but mentioned one of the guys who beat me said "Oh, mistaken identity" they actually thought I was someone else. When they realized I was not the guy, they stopped the brutality and left. When I was safely in the car with my friends, I had a moment of reckoning and was jolted by the truth of that statement and asked myself, 'who was I trying to be'?

I saw that event as a wake-up call and life signalling, I was not being who I really was and if I continued on this path, I would get beat again. I chose to heed the warning that day followed with my standard Thor like battle cry vow, "Oh my God this will never happen to me again!"

Faking it and trying to blend in sucked and I just felt like an imposter. I decided to hit the gym hard and eat as many twenty five cent Big Macs as I could in order to fill out my clothes with my real body. My Mom had briefly dated a guy from the gym and I remember thinking how massive and powerful he looked.

I am sure that is what sparked my interest in reading fitness magazines and going to the gym. I remember being in the gym and working out with such intensity and passion to get bigger and bigger. My goal was to keep the popularity, but lose the multi layers of clothes. Working out and wearing multiple layers of clothes was hot, sweaty and damn uncomfortable at best of times.

During this time, I came to see how trying to fit into the external world was just creating so much more conflict in my life. The more I tried to control, cover up and fix the outside, the more challenges I was given to drive me back internally and deal with my own insecurities. This forced me to stop trying to fit in where I did not belong and start connecting to the power within.

Chapter 10

THE WOLF OF WALL STREET -
LIVING A LIFE OF EXTREMES

There was something lurking inside of me, the Lone Wolf searching for my place in world.

I was married with two little girls. My wife and I struggled to have a healthy relationship and went through many break-ups and reconciliations for the sake of the girls. I felt trapped by loving my daughters so deeply, but I was in so much personal pain and agony. It came to a point when I realized they would be better off without me and I needed to get away from them and stop all the drama and anger. I wanted to start over but didn't even know what that meant.

An opportunity to find out, happened when my wife said they were moving out for good and it really happened. I remember seeing the look on my daughter's small face as she said, "We are going somewhere else to live, but I promise I will come visit you, Daddy."

My heart shattered into a million little pieces as I struggled to come to grips with my new reality. I was losing my family; the ones who were supposed to love me and never abandon me. I couldn't move in those moments. I just stood there in a cold and empty house, watching as they left my life. It felt like I had left my body and was viewing the events unfolding from outside of myself. I fell to my knees and totally broke down as my worst fears had finally come true. I felt like such a failure; a loser and someone who could only ever be abandoned and left alone. I was broken again, and everything was a mess. I found myself back in the same place I had tried so hard to outrun and hide from.

I had given away my power and been pushed to the point where I finally snapped and said "Fuck it!" Everything around me came crashing down. I was sick and tired of pretending to know what the fuck I was doing and how I was supposed to be. I hated my entire environment, from my in-laws, co-workers, and the place I lived. It felt like I was being suffocated as it was all closing in on me.

I didn't care anymore about anything or anyone and especially about being the 'good boy'. In fact, I hated him, I hated his name, I hated how he looked, and I hated how his life was. Something different happened when I was abandoned this time. A trigger was pulled that set off an epic explosion inside, so much so, that what I had always done in the past to cope was completely destroyed.

I rebelled against being good, perfect and trying to blend in. I finally snapped and stopped giving a shit about what anyone else thought of me. I said screw it all and went completely off the rails for a few years, ensuring it was going to be all about me!

Like a warrior, I rose up and charged on into the darkness to take back my power. I allowed myself to rage on and consume like fires of hell and I soon found myself in a fast paced and crazy life of women, money, drugs, alcohol, partying, private jets, guns, strippers and the works. It started after I became completely disgusted with myself for laying in my own pity party on my buddy's sofa for a couple of weeks. I said "Fuck it" and had to do something, so I did. I just knew this time I would be different, and I would use all the skills I had acquired in the past for my own personal gain this time.

I started washing cars for a company with a burning desire to succeed and be recognized. I worked so hard and ingratiated myself so well with the team and management, that they moved me into the office writing contracts. I then became the store manager and eventually the manager for multiple stores in the city. I grew in confidence and my thirst for more expanded so much that I was open to anything.

I became a part of many groups I met in this job; from co-workers, managers, owners and of course some pretty unique and interesting regular customers. They all just let me in and took me along for the ride. I befriended both female and male strippers and partied with them regularly. They were always encouraging me to join them in the industry.

I have to say, the money was awesome and I seriously did consider it. I even went to an audition at one time, but my conscience kicked in and I just couldn't take my clothes off for money. I was taken along on trips in private jets where I partied my ass off, drank my face off and got high on drugs like cocaine and speed. I was burning on the inside and tried to burn it all down on the outside.

I womanized like crazy, having a different girl and car every time I went out. I really liked the younger naïve girls who allowed me to be in control and made it easy for me to not give two shits about them. I learned how to get into the inner circle, be taken along and thrive in this lifestyle. It truly was my time for a good couple of years, until I got a wake-up call to change my direction OR lose my life.

That wake-up moment came when I walked into a party with my new crowd and came face-to-face with an ominous man that I bumped into by mistake. He had a gun, showed it to me and said, "You bumped into the wrong guy and you're in the wrong place and tonight you are going to die, what do you think about that?"

At first, my clever, witty, knee jerk reaction was to say "Well I don't know, no one has ever asked me that question before."

Thank God in a split second I couldn't speak, it was like a big ole Angel had a hold of my tongue! I lightly tapped him on the shoulder in agreement, turned around slowly and slid away. Once I reached the door, I ran out to my vehicle and drove straight home. That moment shook me to my core as I kept replaying the scene over and over again in my mind. I kept hearing the words "You're in the wrong place." This is when I realized I had to change my life, or it would be changed for me.

I was living hard and fast in a lifestyle not meant for me. Nothing ever lasted, had meaning or purpose. Any pleasure there only came from the physical realm and simply vanished the very moment it was realized.

The anger inside me raged on until everything fell apart or was completely destroyed. I thank God for that wake-up call on that day and the opportunity to live on and change it all. At this time in my life, the Lone Wolf was purposeful in showing me who I wasn't and gave me the strength to separate from a life that wasn't serving me. From this I gained focus, drive and insight on how to move forward.

Chapter 11

MY GREAT DEPRESSION

After receiving a lightning bolt to my brain, in the form of a divine wake-up call, I decided to sort myself out, invigorate my ambition and just focus on my career. There was no sense losing my life playing in a lifestyle not meant for me. This time I was going to be true to myself and do the actual work to achieve the success I craved. I was done with just being a tag along. I now wanted my own achievements and performance to validate my worth. When I expressed my intentions to the owners of the franchise and corporate head office, they gave me more and more opportunities to succeed. They entrusted me to manage multiple locations and encouraged all of my ideas and ambition. I felt like I was on top of the world and everything seemed like it was starting to come together, but I was wrong. In the car rental business, we relied heavily on insurance companies, so we did a lot of promoting at conventions and trade shows. On one of these trips to Calgary for an insurance convention, a lady came up to me, introduced herself and said "Hey, I want you to meet my daughter."

I was flattered of course, but at that particular time, I was only concerned about my career and my daughters. I agreed to meet this girl and looking back now, I can see how this became divine intervention. When I met her daughter, I really liked her. She was a nice girl from a good family and well educated. Her and I wound up in a casual long-distance relationship for a couple months, just enjoying telephone conversations and discovering more about each other. Soon after, it would become vividly apparent why we needed to meet that day. Sure enough, a pivotal moment happened to set my life on a new trajectory from which I was on.

While working at a location on the rougher side of the city; I had to deal with a shocking incident. We often had questionable incidences at this location, and it was not uncommon to have drugs, money, booze and other related items left in our cars. This particular situation however, would change my life again. We rented a car to a man, who obviously was involved in a drug deal gone wrong.

He stumbled into our office to return the car with his head cut and bleeding. You could tell that he had been beaten. Our waiting room was full of customers whose jaws were gaping open in shock, as was mine. I wanted to call for help, but the man did not want the cops involved so he ran out leaving our office in a bloody mess. A few days later, some serious gang members came into the office and threatened me. They told me they were going to take care of what happened the other day and the best thing I could do was to forget about it and make myself scarce.

When they left, my mind went wild with all the possible scenarios of what could happen to me. The next week after this incident, a group of credit receivers came into the location and started seizing things. Still rattled from the week prior, I called my bosses and they told me not to worry and it was all a misunderstanding. I was smart enough to know that wasn't true, but how could I not know the company was going out of business? As I handed over the keys to my company car, I was forced to come to grips with the fact my job was ending. Great! No job, no car, now what?

While stunned and still standing amongst the chaos, the phone rang, and it was corporate head office in Calgary to check in and confirm what was happening in the situation. They offered me a job if I was willing to move ASAP. While I was on the phone explaining that I no longer had a car; a car from Vancouver came in that was originally destined for Calgary, but was delivered to us by mistake.

This sort of thing never happens, so I knew this was a sign. I decided to take the job knowing my only regret would be leaving my two daughters behind, but I had to do it, no matter how much it hurt and scared I was. I made a call to my girlfriend in Calgary and she promptly jumped into action saying I could stay with her grandmother until we could figure something out together. Once I settled in Calgary, I fell deeper into a relationship with my girlfriend who was the exact opposite of my first wife.

My first wife was a brunette wild child from a not so good home and upbringing. She was unsettled, angry, emotional and liked to party too much during that time. My new girlfriend was blonde and from a very good, well-educated and wealthy family. She was responsible and had good values. It seemed like I hit the jackpot because I always wanted something that could give me a sense of stability and family. I decided to say yes, fall in line and let her lead the way to a happy life together.

For the next five years, I focused on my career and making money and building my relationship. I was managing a store right away and the boss really took a liking to me. So much so, that within three months, I was an operations manager and learning more about business than I could have ever imagined. It came to a point where I seemed to have the Midas touch, and everything I touched simply turned to gold. After six months or so, I became deeper involved with the company and they really loved my ideas. Soon I became the Sales Manager for Western Canada which had me flying all over and meeting with CEO's, insurance companies and the likes. This was a great time; I was working hard and making more money than I could have ever imagined. I decided to propose to my girlfriend as it felt like it was the right time to get married, buy a home and start a family with her. My daughters really loved her too and gave us their blessing.

About four years in, we had two daughters together and a great lifestyle. I was doing fantastic in my job until one day when I got slapped to the floor with the harsh reality of being an employee. It was decided that I was making too much money in my position. I guess it was ruffling feathers down east, so things had to change.

I was building deeper and stronger sales relationships that led to more business coming in. The company was getting to the point where it did not have enough inventory to keep up with the demand being created and could not risk letting customers down. I had gained so much success and confidence working in this capacity.

Being able to implement my own ideas to help grow the company was a fantastic experience. I really loved building and getting creative so I started working on a new technology that would help the company with on-line bookings to capture more market share. It was supposed to make more money for me too or at least that is what I was led to believe.

Now they were telling me I would have to take a fifty percent pay cut and there would be nothing extra on top of my wage. I remember going into my boss's office and having him tell me I was making too much money. I laughed because I thought in sales that was a good thing because it meant that everybody was doing better. Little did I know, life was going to take another twist. I was being groomed to bloom into an entrepreneur.

Even though I was devastated, I had no choice but to accept the pay cut and suck it up until I could find a better alternative to support my family. During the four months I stayed on, I became extremely aware of how vulnerable I was as an employee and it made me sick. In this job, I had the experience of so much success, freedom and support as an employee. When I look back, this was important because it gave me the confidence to move forward as an entrepreneur when the safety net was ripped away. As I was facing a new storm of emotions, the stress began to mount and take its toll in my relationship and on my family because my lower income simply could not sustain the lifestyle we were used to living.

A friend in Edmonton called me and said he started a new technology business that was making ten thousand dollars a day and he offered me a partnership because it was right up my alley. I immediately jumped at the chance, quit my job and followed my dream of being an entrepreneur. I always wanted to control my own time, income and success. After so many years of being an employee I needed to spread my wings.

My wife however, did not like the idea of the uncertainty or entrepreneurship and pressured me to get a 'real' job. Needless to say, after much bargaining, I ultimately invested our money into the business to pursue my dreams and the dreams I had for my family. This was a risk we were willing to take.

Little did I know this was going to put a wedge between us when the stability and security began to falter. I know it must have felt like I was ripping the rug out from underneath her because all she ever experienced was stability and security of a job. This was new and terrifying for both us.

The business did well at first, but then it stalled and the income started to dry up fast. My business partner jumped ship and later on, I discovered he had a side business without saying a word to me. He kept me in the dark which really pissed me off. Once word got out to our customer base that he was no longer committed to the business, it took a bigger financial hit, and I wound up bringing another business partner on to help keep it afloat.

My mortgage, vehicle, child support and other financial obligations kept on coming. Out of desperation, I placed my trust in the wrong people and got involved in an investment that turned out to be an investment fraud. Our entire life savings of two hundred and fifty thousand dollars was gone and there was nothing I could do about it.

The financial pressure was destroying my marriage. She loved the success and lifestyle we had, but now that it was starting to dissolve, so was her belief in me. We were at the point where she thought the only solution was for me to go up North and work and gave me the ultimatum to do so or they were leaving me. It seemed like a deja vu and I felt all of the same childhood emotions. I felt alone and the fear of being abandoned again.

I had all the memories of my dad leaving, divorce, kindergarten, leaving my kids, losing my jobs and money. It was like a shit storm I could not avoid. It seemed like everything I had built to cover the childhood wounds, to prove my worth, was now being ripped away to expose them again. Feeling like my wife was putting money and security before my needs convinced me she did not love me, so I completely shut down. Unfortunately for my wife and family, from 2007 to 2011, I got enough of a taste of being an entrepreneur and business owner that I could no longer have a choker collar around my neck for someone else to yank on. The marriage fell apart and ended at about the same seven year mark as my first marriage did. My wife took our daughters and moved out in the same way my first wife did.

I was so excited to be an entrepreneur, it was the only area of my life that gave me purpose. My business partner and I were keeping afloat and had ideas of starting another business together. This was a critical time for me. Everything was falling away and all doors in my life were closing except for this one. We were shifting gears from the first business to the second. There was a glimmer of hope and it was a slow start but we both believed in it.

We had to take a shitty room in the back of an automotive shop with mouse crap everywhere and it was so disgusting, but we were solid as partners and I felt confident we would see success soon. My divorce was happening while I was trying to build this second business and it was a bloody nightmare. It felt like I was reliving the same experience I had with my first marriage except it was much worse.

Now, I am not only broke and thirteen years older, but I am over three hundred thousand dollars in debt and my house was being repossessed. My wife was gone, my daughters were gone and my money too. At times I felt as though I could never come back from this place I found myself in. Two ex-wives four kids and now this divorce was threatening the success of my business. The amount of energy and time it was taking with all the lawyers, court dates and other meetings was taking its toll and was gruelling.

All of a sudden I became crazy angry and just wanted somebody to blame. I was so far up shit creek without a paddle it wasn't funny. Being so deep in debt, I wondered how I could get the money to support two families and pay child support for four daughters? I was so angry at God for allowing me to suffer and repeat portions of my parent's lives that traumatized me so badly. Like my loser dad, I also abandoned my kids. I vowed I would never do it and here I did it twice. I was angry at my mom for having two failed marriages. Now I was just like her. What was the point to all of this? All I ever wanted was to be successful and to have someone believe in me, no matter what. I yearned to hear the words "Everything will be OK as long as we are together, we'll get through anything." instead of when things get tough, "I am out of here."

I just wanted to hear "I am with you, I am committed to you and I will never leave you Shawn!" I just wanted the abandonment and being alone to end.

I found myself alone in the house with just my thoughts and emotions. As I contemplated everything in and about my life, the anger and rage welled up and exploded out of me. I started throwing and smashing things and didn't care anymore, how could I?

The house and everything in it would soon be repossessed anyway. I started to think that everyone would be better off without me. I wondered why I never overdosed or why that guy at the party never shot me; he should have. I went from being scared and alone, to angry, then crying over and over again until I finally sat down in front of the fireplace and said to myself "I am not moving until I get to the bottom of this. I am either going to break down and that's the end or I am going to break through."

I decided I was going to die or find the solution on how to move forward without repeating the same patterns. I was tired of building up everything and then ultimately burning it to the ground in the end. When I sat down, I was angry and blamed God and unleashed all the rage there. I also blamed my mother, my father, my brothers and others that I felt were responsible for the pain I was experiencing until I was left with no one else to blame which left me with a blank screen. This is where I finally broke and surrendered.

After a while, I had to accept that no one was coming to save me from the emptiness of the house and deafening sound of silence. I slipped into a depression so deep that days of my life are missing from my memory. I woke up one day with this pain in my side and three days later I could not get out of bed. My wife came to the house and took me to the hospital, out of guilt I am sure, but she showed up nonetheless.

When I arrived at the hospital, they thought I had appendicitis, so they ordered a cat scan and some morphine. After the morphine kicked in, I felt a bit better so while waiting for my results, I sat with the others waiting and we shared our appendicitis stories with each other.

The doctor came to me and said he needed to see me privately which took me by surprise. "Oh God, this was it."

I immediately went into shock and felt myself leave my body and I observed me following him into the room preparing for the worst. He said my organs and supporting tissues were completely inflamed and they needed to do more testing in a couple of weeks.

He gave me Tylenol threes to hold off the pain and sent me home. I was so scared I don't think I would have noticed the pain out of fear. From the moment I got home, I was in so much physical, mental and emotional pain that it was unbearable. I quit giving a shit about the money, the divorce, what anyone thought or even about myself. All I could think about was my four daughters. I wanted to live, I needed to live and have another chance. In that two weeks I surrendered to everything and begged God to tell me what to do and I would do it. I would do anything for my daughters, it was not about me anymore. I just wanted my kids to be happy. I felt like I was being torn apart and something finally broke. It was like all of the identities I had built just shattered; revealing me, the real me, the one who had always been there but just covered up. Finally, I had broken open and could release everything I had inside me. Somewhere, out of nowhere, I heard a voice say, "Now what?"

From this experience I realized falling into a depression was purposeful. It didn't mean it was the end of me, it was simply the end of all the identities that controlled me. That blank screen gave me the opportunity to be in the picture now where I hadn't been before. It felt as though this would be a new beginning and not a repeating pattern.

Chapter 12

LOOKING AT MY REPEATING PATTERNS

Somewhere during my depression I noticed I was able to feel everything and nothing all at the same time. As everything externally began to vanish so did my motivation and desire for anything outside of myself. It was like what I learned and knew as me was dead, yet I felt more alive than ever just being connected me. During the darkest time of my depression, I sat in quiet contemplation waking up at one in the morning every day when it was most quiet. That allowed my subconscious mind to step forward. I allowed my thoughts and emotions to pour out of me and onto the paper or my journal to see what life was trying to show me.

In the morning I would review the beautiful levels of awareness and personal truths I could never have imagined during waking hours of the day. I was getting a glimpse of something magical inside me. I decided to do a life review and become like a coroner performing an autopsy searching for whys and how's. The only way for me to heal was to examine the patterns in my life to gain unconditional love and acceptance that would ultimately set me free. I knew I could not move forward until this was done. I needed to see the repeating patterns and the identities I had created to have an understanding of why these patterns kept repeating.

Anytime I tried to make the source of my success external, it had to fail me to reveal the real truth, which was, I was the source of my own power. I had been covered up and buried in false identities, tainted mindsets and lies. I now understand my dad leaving was purposeful, my mom not being always available to me had its place. Both marriages of seven years and two kids each played a part. The financial success and failures were meaningful and all the physical struggles of acne, glasses, braces, being lanky and awkward were integral puzzle pieces that were part of the journey of transformation.

For the first time, I saw the truth of who I was on the inside and could really feel the purpose of my life now. I was always driven to do more, but it was externally and only in the physical realm. As my awareness grew and I focused on bringing the inside out, I could finally see how these things could have been no other way in order to get me here.

PHASE 2

BUILDING *the* MAN

Chapter 13

THE GREAT TURN AROUND - GOING WITHIN

Realizing on a deeper level, at thirty eight years old, that I could not change, control or fix anything outside of myself, I had to attract a few more experiences just to be sure I got it! I had to really go within and pull my inside out to have life work for me.

In one such experience, I was served a fifty page legal document after my wife and daughters left and I had recovered well enough from my illness to continue to build my business. In those fifty pages was a depiction of a man I didn't recognize. He was a bad father, a terrible husband, a loser and a man who didn't deserve to have his girls. What the fricking hell? I expected the divorce but not this! At that point, I still only wanted to live for my girls, which was the very reason I managed to recover fully, I am sure. Now, my sole reason to live was being threatened to be ripped away from me. How could this be happening?

I had absolutely no money to get a lawyer, but needed one before the court date in six weeks. I obviously wasn't going to accept not being able to see my daughters equally with their mother, regardless of what that fifty page document said about me.

I got busy trying to raise a five thousand dollar retainer. I went to people who owed me money, family, friends and even people I didn't know. I begged for loans, made promises, took in pop bottles and even delivered papers at 2:30 in the morning. I did everything I could until I got the money. When I retained the lawyer; he basically told me it was in my best interest to accept the terms laid out.

He suggested it was standard and not worth the fight for equal rights as the women usually get the kids anyway. He promised to get me every other weekend and I should be happy with that. I fucking wasn't happy with that so I went on another desperate campaign to raise another five thousand dollars to retain a different lawyer, one who would at least try a little harder to give a shit about me and my girls. When I retained that lawyer, I was duped again, they took my money, promised to represent me and then screwed me over when it came time to doing the job. I had no more money when the countdown to the court date started and now, I was worse off! I was in financial ruin. I managed to raise five thousand dollars twice, retain two lawyers, got screwed over and lose it all. Now what? All that effort, struggle and strife for what?

My intentions were so pure and not for myself, but for my girls. As divine intervention would have it, on the last night before court, I secured a lawyer, a woman who really did care, perhaps she was an angel.

I was laying on the bottom of my bunk bed feeling absolutely shitty about everything and just looking up, wishing my girls were in the bunk bed above me. I just wanted them to know how much I loved them and how hard I was trying. As I laid on my bed scrolling through Facebook, I saw a comment from a lady on a post who was a lawyer. In a moment of vulnerability, I reached out to her and she responded to me right away. We wound up having a deep and detailed conversation. I told her my story and she said she would see me at the courthouse the next day. I promised to do anything to pay her and just days later, I received a government refund to start the process.

In court, my wife's lawyer presented first, which was painful and gut wrenching to go through but then my lawyer presented. She explained how hard I was trying to see my girls. I was so happy when we were granted six weeks with no decision. It was a fantastic win for me, but it would also come with a great lesson and a chance to turn it all around.

My lawyer sat me down and in stone cold seriousness she explained in no uncertain terms, how I was going to step up, do everything possible for the girls even when I didn't have the time or think I could. I was going to say what I could not say and do what I could not do and be the Dad I never had with no excuses. If I was willing to do this, then she was confident I would get equal parental rights.

Every day, I drove across the city in rush hour traffic, in the morning and the afternoon just so I could see them and wave as they went in and out of school. Sometimes they didn't see me in the mornings, and I had to convince myself that they did. After school, when they saw me, they would scream for their Mom and say, "We don't want to see him." I was devastated and confused as to why they didn't want to see me; I was their Dad, all I wanted was protect and love them.

Maybe that fifty page document was true, and I was a loser that didn't deserve to have my girls. I would drive off in my car, feeling utterly helpless and ugly cry all the way back to work or home. Every day, I got up and did it all over again because my lawyer said I had to, no matter how hard it was. I needed to prove that I was there for them. For that entire six weeks I kept my word and made my girls a priority over anything else in my life. I showed up when it was inconvenient for me, just to say I loved them, and they kept freaking out, not wanting to see me. I just did what I had to do no matter what and then; it paid off.

I was granted the girls from Thursday to Tuesday. In that time, we rekindled and solidified our bonds to one another. Those days in the park, tucking them in at night and seeing them wake up in the mornings were so beautiful. I would not trade those moments for anything. Later on, I was eventually awarded fifty fifty time with one week on and one week off. This was possible because I never gave up and listened to my inner knowing. I was willing to accept and endure the painful transformation process and be with my daughters.

By listening to my inner voice, I was able to be courageous and take a stand in my life for what I really wanted. This was the beginning of living my life differently. Nobody said having a breakthrough was easy, only necessary. After I was broken in my health, self-worth, relationships and in my finances I came to realize, that the real fight for me was always inside of myself. A switch had flipped and suddenly, I wanted to live differently, deeply rooted in my core values with the newfound power, activated with courage. I wanted to live my life on a higher level in every possible way.

Chapter 14

THE KING - PENTHOUSE OF PERCEPTIONS

At one time in my life, I remember one particular night when I could no longer stand the silence of just sitting in my house. I decided to get out and recharge with some good friends at a nice bar. The beauty of true friends is they are always willing to go out for a few drinks with you and perk you up. The night wasn't anything special really, but what happened, blew my mind and I will never forget it!

The evening started out as any other. We ordered some drinks, caught up on what was going on with each other and just immersed ourselves in the evening. I got up to go to the washroom and when I had come back, I noticed my friends had moved from where we were sitting. I decided to go up to the bar and order a drink and find them after. While I was waiting for my drink, I felt a tap on my shoulder. When I turned around, an old man who had to be about seventy five years old stood there and stared deep into my eyes. At first, I thought he wanted a little more space at the bar to sneak in, so I made room for him and slid over. But then, he tapped me on the shoulder again and this time he locked eyes with me and said, "What is wrong?". What? What the heck was he talking about? Nothing was wrong, I was just getting a drink. Geez, what's with this guy? Because he came out of left field like that, I just stood there stunned for a moment before I really looked into his piercing eyes and noticed something. His eyes were full of life, love and something else indescribable and for a moment I got lost, until he asked again "What is wrong?" I impulsively responded by saying there was nothing wrong, in fact, I was great. He told me he knew what I was going through and it was time to change. Ok, now that was fricken weird coming from a complete stranger. I then noticed how quiet things became and how well I could hear him. It was like we had a soundproof space of our own. Normally in this bar, you could barely hear yourself think let alone hear anyone else talk without yelling. Here we were, connecting in a space with pin drop silence. He said, "I can see you are suffering and confused, I have been there also and would like the opportunity to help you." Obviously, this was not the place, so he handed me his business card, asked me to call him and then just slipped away. I looked at his card and quickly put it into my wallet. I was totally dumbfounded, I decided to leave as well. As I drove home, contemplating what just happened I realized my biggest life lessons were often foreshadowed with interesting moments like this.

The next day, I woke up drowning in anxiety and with the same problems I had hoped to escape with my friends at the bar. I could not get that man out of my mind, let's call him Fred, he really left a lasting hold on me and I could not shake that experience. A couple days later, I was inspired to call him, so I did. Fred answered and said, "I'm really glad you called, would you like to talk and have a coffee"? I told him that sounded like a really good idea as I was in need of some guidance. He said he lived in a downtown building and that it would be more suitable if I came there to visit him. He said to park around back and take the elevator to the top floor. When I got there, I parked my car, got in the elevator and was brought up to the penthouse suite where he lived. When the elevator door opened, it revealed the entirety of his home. The whole top floor of that building was his space alone. He was there to greet me with a big smile on his face and as I walked in, I couldn't help but be amazed and bewildered. He asked me if I liked what I saw and I said, "Yeah this is beautiful." He chuckled and said he thought I might like the view. Then he said, "I wanted to give you an experience of something firsthand, now walk over to the window and tell me what you see." The breathtaking view of the entire city was amazing, and I felt on top of the world in that moment. I told him it was stunning, beautiful and magnificent. He said "Right! The view from the top is absolutely amazing. Now look down on the ground and tell me what you see. I saw a guy going through the dumpster looking for food and another guy who was sleeping right next to the dumpster. I felt so sad and disheartened bearing witness to that scene. Fred told me life on this higher level of surrender is completely different than on the lower levels of resistance. Even though right below us is suffering and struggle, the view from this position is beautiful and quite amazing. Where you are right now may be a place of suffering and struggle, but you just need to level yourself up and change the perspective of where you are coming from. You stop fighting what is and let go of resisting what you don't want. A switch flipped inside my head and my mind was blown. In that moment, I decided to drop the ideas of chasing money to solve all my problems from a lower level. Fred just showed me I could come from a higher perspective with a new intention to level up my life, just as I was, right here and right now. As the saying goes, "When the student is ready the teacher will appear". I was definitely ready, and Fred made a mystical appearance as my teacher.

I poured out my entire story to Fred, I left nothing out. I had hoped it would help him understand me and why I lost almost everything in my life twice including my self-esteem and pride. After listening to me, Fred said, "Don't fight it, let it go". I told him I couldn't' just let it go as I was already in the midst of a legal battle and could not risk losing my girls and everything else, like I did the first time. What he meant, was don't fight the circumstances meant to hone you, let go of the resistance to the situation. He told me to look beyond my current circumstances and encouraged me to move forward and re-create my life from a place of peace. His suggestion was to not forget about the things in the material world but intensify the connecting to myself on a deeper level. He believed the power was in your peace and the peace is in your power. What he meant by that was you can have the most amazing experience and be happy no matter where you are and what is going on around you. I replied by saying yes but in the end, I lost it all anyway even if I was to be peaceful. I didn't get what I wanted. Fred looked at me seriously and said, "And here you are again, do you want to end this pattern in your life once and for all?" He said if I was willing to trust and allow him to teach me, he could help me find that peace within. I showed up looking for solutions to my problems, not for a psychology session what the hell?

Fred mentioned he had gone through similar experiences with divorce and money. He had also been instructed to fight and protect everything at all cost to not be taken advantage of. Fred chose instead, to give it all up so he could be at peace and move forward with his life rather than be stuck the quicksand pulling him down. I could not even imagine what my life would look like if I had given up without a fight. I would have lost my girls, my will to live and had to immense shame to for the rest of my life. Because I fought, I got my girls and the validation that I was worthy on some level to have them. I didn't understand how the fight was not worth the financial ruin. I knew I could always make more money, but I could never have more time with my girls. I was interested to see what he had to say about that. Fred sat me down to explain how the peace inside of me was more powerful to create my future as opposed to the anxiety and turmoil. He explained to me that life is like a mirror reflecting what's on the inside of yourself. Yes, I needed to do everything I could to defend and protect my rights to have my daughters but only if I could come from a place of inner peace. In order to have success, personal freedom, joy and abundance, I would need to come from that higher level. He said to me, my life changed because I lived this principal and he wanted the same for me.

Fred showed me the most amazing places he had traveled to and shared the life lessons he received in each one. I remember this one story he shared about a rain forest and the lesson was remaining present and calm when the first reaction was to panic. He mentioned how the indigenous people would dip their arrowheads into the extracts of certain poisonous plants to hunt with. It was extremely deadly to be handling such noxious plants, but the indigenous people knew if they remained calm and peaceful, their presence of mind and spirit would show them the natural antidote to that toxin. They knew the forest was set up in such a way that within a three foot radius, what was needed could be found. The most successful and powerful warriors were those who did not panic but rather, tapped into their peace and presence of mind in order to stay focused and provide well for their tribe. Just before our conversation ended, Fred emphasized that it wasn't the end goal that was all the that mattered, it was the process between where I was and where I wanted to end up. All the power is in the intention of first step and every step after that one on this journey. It was about being present in every moment, right here, right now. When I left, I went away contemplating our many hours together that impacted and shifted my mindset. In the days the followed I felt as though there was a shift which led to me see the world in a different way. I was able to cut the anchors of what was holding me back so I could rise the next level.

Several weeks went by since our first meeting and conversation. It generated so many burning questions that needed to be answered. Looking for clarity, I decided to call Fred. A message came on saying the number I was calling was no longer in service. Since I was in the area, I drove over to see if Fred was home. When I arrived at the building, I wasn't allowed to go up to his home. The security guard told me the penthouse was now vacant which left me shocked and dumbfounded. Just like that, I was left with more questions than answers and now, this amazing mystery man was gone from my life. The only thing I had was the knowledge that Fred imparted on me in that short time we had together. I will forever remember his words, "Your power is in your peace and presence." That day, I made a conscious decision to hold on and apply the principals he taught me to find that inner peace and power he wished for me.

Chapter 15

BECOMING THE FITNESS MODEL

What I yearned for most was a complete transformation. I began to get a sense that if I could transform my body, I could also transform my life. This is what took me into the field of fitness. I wanted nothing more than to tap into the power and potential held inside and allow it to express its full magnificence in every aspect of my life. Initially I dove into fitness to regain the energy I lost and to get healthy. I still remember the day I snapped at my daughter. When she looked up at me with tear filled eyes it broke me inside.

That is when I realized I need to get more energy to be the dad I wanted to be. I also had the burning desire to look good so I could feel better about myself. I wanted to change my soft round dad body. In the past, I noticed whenever I felt good about myself, things just naturally seemed to go my way. I wanted to live a more powerful life. After a couple of weeks, when the focus on myself began to grow and intensify, I would use my workouts to build the connection to myself.

One day while doing a workout, I was approached and asked if I was going into a fitness competition. He said it looked like I was really slimming down. I said no I wasn't, but that was interesting. Over the next couple days, two more people said I should compete because it looked like I would do well. One of them even gave me the card of a trainer that specialized in fitness competitions. I took the card and was wise enough to know this series of events was another sign for me to take action.

I called the gym and the trainer invited me to come and talk about fitness on a higher level which really intrigued me. I wondered what he meant by a higher level. When I arrived, I felt so uncomfortable and as funny as it seems right now, having to pay two dollars and fifty cents for parking every time triggered me to question whether or not this was the right thing to do, considering my circumstances. I even stopped, turned around and retreated back to my car. As I sat there, squeezing the steering wheel and feeling like a complete idiot, I heard that inner voice say to me "Now what?"

If a mere two dollars and fifty cents is enough to set you back, then what else will be able to block you? Oh my God! Seriously, I thought, you're right, almost anything could stop me if I let it. So, I sorted myself out, wrangled up the fears and insecurities and coaxed them with as much confidence I could muster to get my ass out of the car and into that gym.

When I walked in, I immediately felt judged and like an imposter that didn't belong there. By now, I was experienced enough to recognize that it was just my own issues coming back up to greet me and say hello. I simply acknowledged those feelings and put them to rest. I reminded myself to not back down from my fears and just push through them. I thought about my daughters; why I was doing this and signed up with this new gym to train for a fitness competition.

About halfway home, buyer's remorse began to set in. What the hell was I thinking? I had no money, was up to my eyeballs in debt and here I go and slam my credit card. I managed to brush off the second guessing by convincing myself I had a few days to change my mind and could cancel without a problem. The next day I woke up and resolved to not let my old ways sneak back in and undermine me. I started my new training, complete with very structured workouts and a meal plan that was so clean, it had me wondering if I could do it, but I did. I totally dove in and embraced it all, knowing someday it would all be worth it, and it was.

The more I prepped my food and trained hard, my negative thoughts and emotions would try to slink in and expose some fears and doubts. I was extremely strict and committed to the plan and keenly aware there was a war going on inside of me. What if I could do this? And what if I couldn't? The good thing was, I saw amazing physical results only after two weeks, nothing was going to stop me, or so I thought. This fitness journey gave me something I could control, while learning about commitment, discipline, dedication and consistency because I had to work out every day no matter what.

I needed to eat in a certain way and at exact times, regardless of what thoughts and feelings came up. I wasn't just changing my body, I was actually changing my entire life. I faced every fear and insecurity I ever held about my own body image and came to terms with the fact I would be stepping forward, practically naked in front of so many people expecting to be judged so I could get my pro card. I literally was inviting for the first time in my life, judgement and I was actually stoked about it.

This personal transformation period was six months long and consisted of hard core, everyday trainings. I put it all on the line to transform my body to the point where I lost fifty five pounds and built big, well-sculpted and defined muscles you could see without flexing. People began to notice me a lot more now and it was great validation, but it simply wasn't enough to protect me from my own self sabotage, was it? You know it!

Two weeks before the competition, I had an emotional breakdown of epic proportions because I allowed what other people thought of me to get in to my inner thoughts. I immediately reverted to old ways and sped to Tim Hortons like an F1 race car driver. I ordered a large double double and a blueberry muffin, because that had always been my go-to and routine.

All of a sudden, when the sugar and caffeine hit my system, I became like a drug addict who needed more and more immediately. Because I was far too embarrassed to go back into the Tim Hortons drive thru, I drove two blocks away to McDonalds, where I ordered a milk shake, burgers and a McFlurry. Even though I was feeling such weakness and was covered in shame, I wasn't done yet. I couldn't stop myself, I literally was out of control. I found the nearest Dairy Queen and ordered a blizzard and a burger. I guess if I was going to cheat, I was going to go the absolute extreme; like I have done with most things in my life.

After this complete and total meltdown I sat there in my car filled with guilt, regret and disgust of what just happened. The five and a half months of hard work just evaporated in my mind and I felt defeated. I called my coach to confess. I know he meant well, but it didn't help when he tried to cheer me up. I knew deep inside that I really messed up and I wanted nothing more than to redeem myself. I took the next week and a half to undo the massive sugar, salt and carb load in my body, but I couldn't seem to get rid of the guilt and shame that lingered and ate me up inside.

For the competition, I had to fly into Montreal, and of course, as shit luck would have it, I chose the wrong damn airport to fly into. This mistake was a four hour cab ride to the right venue. By the time I arrived, I had let the frustration consume me and I couldn't bounce back in my attitude. Even though I was excited to get on stage and still looked fantastic, I only got third place that day, which sucked and stung my ego pretty good. The first and second place people got their pro cards and I didn't which felt like a sucker punch to the gut. I had hoped to come back with that ever coveted pro card in my hands, but I didn't.

I was really down in the dumps about not getting the pro card at this competition and just felt empty inside. My coach came and asked me "Now what?"

Oh those oh so familiar words… "Now what?"

As we talked things out, he mentioned that we had six weeks to train more and fly to Vancouver for another chance to compete.

If we didn't jump now, I would have to wait months for another opportunity. I was so angry at myself that I just blurted out "Let's do Vancouver" and I will pull together six more weeks of pure dedication and ensure nothing would stop me from getting my pro card this time. Well guess what?

The very same weekend of the competition was my daughter's high school graduation. Oh my God, are you kidding me? Shit! Why couldn't I have done it right the first time? Crap! Now what? Great! You know what I was in for with the family right? My daughter really wanted me to be there for her and I wanted that too, but why in the hell did it have to be on the same day as my competition, that I took six months to train for?

Both my exes, who were now very close to each other by then, my daughters and the in-laws were not shy about expressing how self-indulgent they thought I was, to put this competition ahead of her graduation.

I was stuck between a rock and a hard place with my daughter and the opinions of everyone else. I threw my hands in the air and begged for an answer. I was on my knees again praying for an answer, but nothing came. No one could even imagine where I was coming from. This wasn't just a fitness competition for me, this was my life and I had put everything on the line to compete there.

I had already been judged, weighed and measured as a man, in front of a crowd of people, almost naked, on a stage which was such a victory for me on so many levels. Now I was faced with this very tough decision. Either way, I could not win. I was going to hurt someone no matter what decision I made. I was positive I could not continue to be in training for many more months to enter the next competition. It would mean continuing to workout every day, meal planning and eating one hundred percent clean. It was expensive, time consuming and quite frankly, I was powering out. I just felt like nobody could understand me or what it took for me to do this.

Shortly after this graduation upset, my daughter Sophie, for Father's Day, made and coloured me a picture and wrapped it around a chocolate bar. It said secret identity bar, when you eat this, you turn into the superhero you are.

In that moment, I knew I had the power to face everyone and make the best choice for me. I also realized this is what I would want my daughters to do in life as well.

Make the tough decisions when they had to and choose their happiness first. I knew if I made a choice which would leave me with feelings of resentment or guilt, I needed to choose guilt because at least I was taking care of myself. I talked with my daughter and she understood what was on the line for me and I got her blessing and support to go and compete. That night, I won first place and got my pro card. My first phone call was to her to say I won my pro card. I broke down in tears and felt like I had pulled off a miracle and at the same time, I was so sad I couldn't have been there for her, but it wasn't because I didn't love her.

What I learned at that time was how to put my own wants and needs first and still be able to handle all the challenges and obstacles that came my way. I hadn't figured it out yet, but I was seeing there was another way to live my life.

Chapter 16

THE WARRIOR - TAKING A STAND

I discovered deeper integrity when I was training a client. She was only interested in the surface level of fitness and only wanted to do what was easy or convenient. I always demanded a one hundred percent commitment and expected that she would, like me, do whatever it took to achieve the fitness goal we set together. Looking back, I should have never convinced her to work with me. Each and every session was almost a living hell as she resisted and complained about everything. With each session that passed, I felt I needed to have *the talk* with her. For my own character and integrity to be intact, I needed to have the talk and give her the chance to either step up and meet me on the next level or I needed to fire her, because she was draining my energy. There were only two sessions left with her, so I thought maybe I would just ride it out and finish the sessions.

This way, I didn't have to instigate any negativity and she could just go her own way after that. I should have known better. I was about to get a hard lesson in integrity and tough choices. My client had been out partying the night before, so she came in apathetic and grumbling. I decided to take it easier on her due to her state. As she was doing box jumps and not focusing like she needed to, she wound up miscalculating her jump and landed on the lip of the box.

Instead of falling forward like she was taught, she curled up into a ball and started to fall backwards. Instinctively, I reached out to catch her with one arm. My arm snapped back and as it did, my bicep tendon tore, releasing my bicep to roll up towards my shoulder. Luckily this was at the end of her session with me. I literally just slinked away and wondered if she even realized what had happened to me. I was so pissed off with myself. I was in excruciating pain and was rushed to the hospital where I saw a surgeon.

The nurses immediately started prepping me for surgery. As this was happening, I realized there was a huge problem. I was supposed to compete on the Worlds stage against the top pro fitness competitors from all over the world in eight weeks.

As I stared down at my arm, a voice inside told me to just relax and pay attention. Upon further examination, this surgeon decided he wanted me to see a sports injury specialist first.

I was relieved for that moment and just prayed the damage could be repaired. Two days later I saw the specialist and he said I would most definitely require surgery due to the fact that there was only one tiny thread of tendon holding my bicep in place. He expected that would snap in the next few days and then he could do the surgery for me because it would be easier to unroll it and attach it all at once.

By now I was getting really good at listening to this inner voice and trusting it more and more as opposed to freaking out and having knee jerk reactions to the situations I found myself in. From a place of calm, I told him I was competing on the Worlds stage in eight weeks and maintained my composure as he laughed and said I would be off for a year and probably not be able to compete again due to the severity of the injury. Inside, I knew there had to be another option, I just knew it and I wanted to see if I could do anything to help this situation before surgery. He said he would schedule me an appointment to see a specialist, which bought me some time and I had nothing to lose.

The next day, I went to the gym to assess myself and see where I was at. I knew my own body, how it moved and definitely how to take care of myself. I picked up a two pound dumbbell and after two reps I knew that small thin thread was going to snap, so I stopped immediately and realized it was serious. But in the coming days as I went back to the gym, ever so carefully doing small rep after rep and other exercises, I experimented on how to position and engage the muscles and supporting tissues differently, to tap into my body's own wisdom and ability to heal itself. I was able to tap into a new of level of consciousness.

Day after day I went back to the gym and paid close attention to my body and listened to what it needed. I went from two pound dumbbells to five pounds to ten pounds to fifteen to twenty pounds for my arms. I actually started hearing that voice inside guide and coach me along the way on how to heal and build it back. At the two week mark, I started to believe competing in six weeks was actually possible. With each passing week, I was getting stronger and my bicep was repositioning itself. It was like I was retraining the cellular memory of that bicep to go back to the way it was before the trauma. My surgeon was literally blown away. He had no idea how this was possible and how I was able to heal myself. He literally said to me "You are actually teaching me something new."

Inside, I could feel the warrior develop as an inner truth rose up with a different level of intensity. It was challenging my own limiting beliefs; what society experts said was possible. In the past, I was always seeking the approval and advice of others, never really thinking to go within and take instruction from my own inner wisdom.

This was the first time I could see what brilliance and magnificence was available for me to tap into. I became so focused, intent and technical with my workouts that fitness magazines took notice and wanted to know the story.

The fitness people watched in amazement as day by day I built my body back to be even stronger than before the injury. I had a completely different mind-set. What's interesting is, I was also training a few guys for their first fitness competitions in order for them to get their pro cards. Because of the difference in mindsets, they allowed a few simple aches and pains to derail them from their focus and training. Ultimately this led to them pulling out of the competition and running straight for pizza and Ben and Jerry ice cream for comfort. I knew the spot they were in and could totally relate to how they were feeling. They let it get the better of them and quit.

As word got out, a few fitness magazines asked to interview and feature me in their publications. I was also asked to speak at a few men's groups and entrepreneur networking events.

I shared the message of being an enlightened warrior who is always ready to take on challenges and face insurmountable odds, by staying connected to a higher purpose and being guided from within. I shared the importance of having unwavering goals and learning to activate natural talents and develop the skills necessary to achieve a level 10.

Just two weeks before the competition I dug deep into my mind, body and warrior spirt to ground myself and be ready for it. This was the best of the best competitors from all over the world. When the time finally arrived, I stepped on stage and I was overcome with emotion. It finally hit me as to what I was able to pull off in eight weeks, which was nothing short of a miracle. With a newfound awareness and inner strength, I not only placed Top Ten in the World, but I held my Top Ten World ranking in what could have been a career ending injury if I had let it. Not only that, I was competing as a 44 year old against competitors half my age and proud to say I did it completely natural with no performance enhancing drugs.

In this time, I formed a new allegiance to myself and I discovered a deeper meaning of character and integrity and connected to my core values which ultimately gave me clarity and a renewed purpose.

Chapter 17

THE MYSTIC - LIVING IN THE MYSTERY

In an earlier chapter, I talked about meeting Fred. In this chapter, I'd like to share more about that experience and what else I learned from him. So here goes.

After my experience with Fred in the penthouse, I began an exhaustive search for meaning and purpose in my life. I wanted to be connected and grounded in the peace he spoke about so I could experience the power to level up my life. I had so many unanswered questions and clearly, I was ready for another transformation. While battling it out in court and in the locker room at the gym, I gravitated to the church in the hopes my answers could be found there.

A girl I met at the gym was the one who got me involved in the church, she said it would help me understand the messes I created and know God's purpose for my life. That was music to my ears and all I ever wanted to know. What was the meaning and purpose to the life I was living?

I saw meeting her as a sign and decided to go to church following the guidance from the universe once again. Well, because I am who I am, I got highly involved and committed, giving one hundred percent effort to the church. After all, I had a lot of years to make up for. I remember dragging my daughters there every Sunday and studying one-on-one with the pastor, partaking in a free apprenticeship type program that was accelerated from one and half years to a few months. Every day for four hours, I would study with the pastor; story by story and line by line in the bible. It was not easy, as the bible had to be perceived and interpreted to understand the meaning. It was great being able to sit with the pastor and find meaning in the teachings we read each day. He wanted to teach me, and I wanted to find the purpose of my life. I never experienced anything like this growing up and it was filling a void and giving me comfort.

This intense bible study went on for three months and ran parallel with my commitment at the gym. I was learning and seeing things in a whole new way from all the teachings in the bible. Everything was going along so well, until one day, I mentioned to my pastor, I would be entering a fitness model competition and that was my reason for being at the gym every day. I honestly thought he'd be supportive but that was not the case.

His whole demeanor changed, and my fate was sealed in that moment. My time at the church had come to an abrupt end. He would not support me in this religion if I was going to compete on stage like that. Just like that, I was kicked out. This left me feeling very bitter and I was devastated again. Everything I learned about compassion, acceptance, non-judgement and love from the stories in the bible didn't seem to apply to me apparently. Wow, I couldn't even gain acceptance in a church where everyone is welcome and loved by God. It became all too much for me to handle, the only thing I could do was think, are you kidding me? Right now, and laugh at the hilarity of it knowing I was being prepared for something else.

I had met another girl later on who said going to church never really worked for her, but she belonged to this amazing spiritual group that was very low key, shrouded in mystery and was almost like a secret club. I was intrigued. She said I would learn the secrets of life from the non-denominational and spiritual aspect as opposed to the more rigid traditional religions.

Oh wow, I thought, this is perfect for where I was right now. So I decided to go to the breakfast meeting and find out more. After attending a few meetings, I was instantly hooked on this new way of seeking spirituality. I started learning meditation to quiet my mind and how to go within myself. I was learning how to contemplate and process my emotions which was helping me come to understand how to embrace the power in the peace that Fred taught me. I often felt Fred had actually led me there to help me integrate his teachings. For a while, this was a beautiful experience but then the demands of this became more than I could handle. I was getting a lot of push back for wanting to live life my way.

I was working out really hard at the gym and trying to run and build a business. I never realized how difficult it was to sit on the floor cross legged for fifteen minutes, let alone an hour that I was supposed to work up to. After a few months, the expectation came that I needed to sit in mediation twice a day for an hour. They assigned me a bunch of books to read and be quizzed on. I was catching flack because I was falling behind and failing miserably. I started to wonder who in the hell has this kind of time to do all this reading and meditation?

How was I going to go to the gym, build a business and have any time or energy left for my daughters or anything else in my life? They really didn't seem to care about what I wanted for my own life. It seemed as though they just wanted me to fit into their rule box, which I couldn't, so I got kicked out of this place too for not showing integrity with their methodology. Oh well, here we go again I thought and wondered what life had in store for me next.

During this time, I attended marriage and family counselling with my soon to be ex-wife. I tried as hard as I could to keep my family together, but I just couldn't fit into the box she created for me. The freedom to be an entrepreneur and fully express my life was more important than trying to please someone else at the expense of who I was. I was no longer prepared to be a yes man and subscribe to the philosophy happy wife, happy life. What about my life and what I wanted? Why did everyone need me to be in a box and keep me small anyway?

During the same time, my business partner and I were just starting to get some really good business traction with our new company and I was so excited. We were not really making any money to speak of at the time, but we sure were making connections and had just enough funding to build out the technology for insurance companies. We were even approached by another company looking to acquire us. It was an exciting time and I thought I found my identity and place in business again. My business partner and I decided to bring in some new partners to help us scale up the business. They brought with them, fantastic experience from Silicon Valley and knew how to position us in the market for a larger sale. After some time, we had the company valuated and came in at just over 3 million dollars. I felt this new rise in value would lead to certain success and just at the right time in my life. We had struck a deal to sell after much negotiating that was contingent on us completing the deal with the insurance company, we designed it for. Unfortunately, when it came to signing on the dotted line, the insurance company backed out and did not go into contract with us. So, in less than twenty four hours our deal went bust and slipped away. From then on, our company started to spiral down. Both my partner and I were devastated. We literally had to rebuild the company to suit another insurance client, which we did and then decided to keep the company. What I was noticing is that life was flowing faster and through me as I was giving up control. When I let go of the fight and resistance, peace and presence became real.

The teaching here, is about real integrity to your purpose and allowing life to flow through you. There is a real power in surrender and not trying to know how everything will unfold. For the first time, I could understand the words I had been hearing in my head "What's next?"

I learned to trust life and how to go with the flow step by step with life, so it could unfold faster than it ever had before. I was ready to get out of my own way.

Chapter 18

WHAT'S THE STORY LINE YOU HAVE BEEN LIVING?

Through all my experiences and situations, I came to understand in order to heal the boy, I needed to acknowledge the pain. According to Jim Rohn, "We cannot heal what we cannot feel." It was in seeing the innocence of the boy that I could step forward and embrace the boy seeing wholeness and perfection that allowed the healing to happen. This was the beginning of building the bridge over troubled waters between healing the boy and building the man. It's key to know the pain, and confusion the little boy felt is still there, it has not been resolved. The inner boy is living very much inside waiting to get our attention. I didn't come into this life with courage I had to build it! Brick by brick I had to face each challenge as an opportunity to prove, that we as human beings have more power and potential inside than any obstacle we may face. Ultimately it revealed the man I have become today.

Life is always mirroring back opportunities to know your true identity with all the circumstances and situations you find yourself in. There is nothing to face or conquer outside of yourself. When you become aware and accept the greatness within, you can take action from a peaceful power and transform your life. You never have to struggle, prove or feel broken again. You are enough.

In the childhood wounding process, it may have seemed like something vital was snatched away forever. This is why you created identities and versions of the truth from which to operate. Everything you believed was lost or stolen has, in fact, been kept safe for you to reclaim once again. The wounds of the past do not define you; they build you. You never came into this world to simply heal old childhood wounds, you came here to transform because of them.

May you embrace and connect to the entire story of your own life, the good, the bad and the ugly. To see and understand how the lessons that come through challenges are like chapters in a book, designed to make you stronger.

Life's purpose was always to masterfully prepare you for your destiny, by developing you within so you could share your unique gifts, talents and treasures with the world. Your purpose is to tap into and connect with the unlimited power planted within. It's exactly like the acorn that holds the blueprint to reach the full potential of the mighty oak. All you need to do is embrace what is, show up completely and do all that you can, to create the life you truly want. All the while, coming from that place of peace and presence to let life flow through you.

Getting to the next level is always just around the corner of your next challenge. When you learn to come from your higher vision and purpose, life will open up and support you living your best life ever and reaching your level 10 potential.

Chapter 19

WHAT HAS HAPPENED SINCE THE AGE OF 38 TO 46?

In fitness, after winning my pro card I continued on my journey and went on to compete and become the North American Champion, all natural (no performance enhancements) I might add. My competitors at that time were half my age and pumped on steroids and I won the title. At the age of forty I became an international fitness cover model and then did it again at the age of forty six, which is really unheard of. I have been interviewed many times over, written articles for fitness magazines and was even a columnist for Entrepreneur and other business magazines. I now have an expansive network of amazing people and a social media following that keeps on growing. I created and designed a fitness technology to go along with my level 10 training program. I brought in business partners to leverage my time so I could offer a higher level of personal training to those individuals willing to commit and invest one hundred percent.

This one on one training with me is for those who want more than just a meal plan and workout program. I am committed to helping others align to their own destiny. Going forward, I see being able to connect to and support more people in their journey of healing and connecting to their purpose.

In business and finances I went from creating a multimillion dollar business idea on a napkin to a national company in the insurance industry in just over a year. I have been able to duplicate that scenario with another business in the same industry, and create a million dollar business in the fitness and personal development world. Right now my life is fantastic. I have been able to leverage my time so I could free up some personal time to spend with my family and have time for myself.

In my personal relationship with my wife I can say I have found my true soul mate. We met in the fitness industry, as we were both personal trainers and competitors as fitness models. She was cracked open just like me and made it through the other side. She believes in the real me and we are best friends. All the relationships I have with my children are loving and supportive.

My goal for you is to find a way to heal your inner child and build yourself into the strong adult you want to be.

MY 10 GUIDING PRINCIPLES

So how do I be "ME" when I have multiple businesses, do speaking engagements, write articles and now books, physically train myself for fitness competitions, coach clients and run a busy family of six kids AND stay balanced? It's not easy, and it's not perfect; and I have never been healthier, wealthier, and truly happier!

I get asked all the time, what does my life look like now?

In one sentence this is it, "I put my inner peace and power above anything on the outside and I've learned through my journey, that my life is about *healing the boy and building the man*."

I live by my 10 Guiding Principles.

Words of Wisdom to My Younger Self - the Boy Within

10 Guiding Principles

1. There's a PERFECT FIT within, but don't be shy about STANDING OUT!

2. You get to LEAD your own life but remember to FOLLOW your own HEART!

3. Take a STAND for UNDERSTANDING yourself and your life… but SURRENDER your resistance also!

4. Say YES to your Inner Yes, MORE than the desire to say yes to the external material world! (Especially other People)

5. Become the GENERATOR in your life by GIVING what's missing! (give love, confidence, commitment, courage first to yourself, then to others)

6. ASK MORE from YOURSELF (your true essence) than anyone else can ask from you!

7. Don't get COMFORTABLE in life and don't let anything in life BOTHER you!

8. Turn the SHIT of life into the FERTILIZER for your GROWTH!

9. It's not what's WRONG in your life, it's WHAT'S NEXT!

10. Become a VISION HOLDER, not just a Problem Solver.

ABOUT THE AUTHOR

Shawn T. McIntyre spent 38 years of struggling with health issues, two failed marriages and bankrupt businesses when one day sleeping on his best friends couch, began to see life's challenges had been setting him up - not to fail but succeed at the highest level!

Within 2.5 short years, Shawn turned around a -300,000 debt load to creating a million dollar company, becoming an International Cover Model and totally turning his entire life around.

Shawn is now teaching, speaking around North America inspiring, hope, belief and education to Top Executives, Entrepreneurs, Doctors, Lawyers and High Achievers how to live and love in your true strength and create your UNSTOPPABLE LIFE!

THE FINAL NOTE

One final note, I'd like to say is this. When I first started writing my book, I wanted to title it, 'Unstoppable' because that seemed to be my life. It seemed like a great fit, until my editor Karen Michele West, and I started working together on the book. She said "Shawn, you mentioned something that won't leave me, what do you think about Heal the Boy, Build the Man as your book title?"

I loved it! And said "Yes! That's it!"

And then my publisher, Kelly Falardeau said, "Shawn why don't you include a photo of your son, Theo James looking into the mirror and seeing himself as a man, which would be you. That way you have the younger version of you as the boy and the older version of you as the man."

And so, you guessed it… Theo James my son, is the boy on my cover.

Why does this mean so much to me? As I watch my son grow up, I think to myself, is he going to turn out like me? Is he going to go through the challenges I went through in my own life? Is he going to be bullied like I was? Is he going to go through two failed marriages to finally find the love of his life? Is he going to be held at gun point? Is he going to get hooked on drugs and alcohol? Is he going to meet his own version of 'Fred' that will help him transform his life? What is my own son Theo going to live through so he can build his manhood and become an unstoppable man like me?

One thing I know for sure, I will be a strong father figure to my son and help him through his own journey in life. He will become his own version of himself, living through his own journey of life to become a man. Theo, I am here for you now and I promise, I will be the father I always longed to have in my own life so you can become a strong man.

Contact Shawn for speaking engagements, coaching, fitness modelling, articles, etc at: www.ShawnTMcIntyre.com

Manufactured by Amazon.ca
Bolton, ON